MAZE ★ MANIA

Written, illustrated, and designed by

Patrick Merrell

Troll

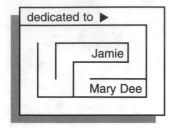

dedicated to ▶

Jamie

Mary Dee

This new edition published in 2001.

Copyright © 1996 by Patrick Merrell.

Published by Troll Communications L.L.C.

Printed in the United States of America.   ISBN 0-8167-4111-5

10 9 8 7 6 5 4 3 2

Welcome,

maze meisters. I am Dr. Knotts and this is my Labyrinth Lab. I have been tuning up the Maze Machine in preparation for our journey—a journey in search of mazes. And not just the usual scribbled scrawl of paths and pits—not those ho-hum heaps of lifeless lines. No, we're going in search of the mysterious. The mesmerizing. The monumental. The mind-bogglingly marvelous. Prepare yourselves for...

Maze★Mania

Care to join me? Of course you would. Why else would you have this book in your hands!

1 WHAT KNOTTS

It appears I've forgotten to properly introduce myself. You know my last name—Knotts— but not my first. Many people assume it is Doctor, but it is not. Following the arrows, can you find the one route that will take you from "Start" to "End"? The letters along that route will spell out my first name:

__ __ __ __ __ __

2 UNDER THE HOOD

Before we leave the lab, perhaps you could help me. In my rash rush to repair the Maze Machine, it seems I've gotten a few of my widgets and wires crossed.

On the next page, I need to find out which lever starts the engine, which activates the wheels, which controls the maze-o-scope, which honks the horn, which operates the radar detector, and which runs the toaster oven. Got any idea?

Write down the number of the lever that activates each feature:

____ **Engine Starter**

____ **Wheel Activator**

____ **Maze-o-scope Controls**

____ **Horn**

____ **Radar Detector**

____ **Toaster Oven**

SEIZE THE KEYS

I need the keys to the Maze Machine. There are four keys below, but only two of them are for the Maze Machine (they are marked with an "MM"). Can you find a route that will pick up both "MM" keys and neither of the others?

CHALK IT UP

If there's one thing I've learned in all my years of scientific hobnobbery, it's this:
  1. Have a plan.
  2. Remember your keys.
On the chalkboard on the next page I have plotted several ways to get across town. Starting at "Start" and ending at "End," can you figure out a route that will make one stop at each of the six places shown?

Travel Bonus:

When you're done with that, can you find *two* routes that each make exactly three stops?

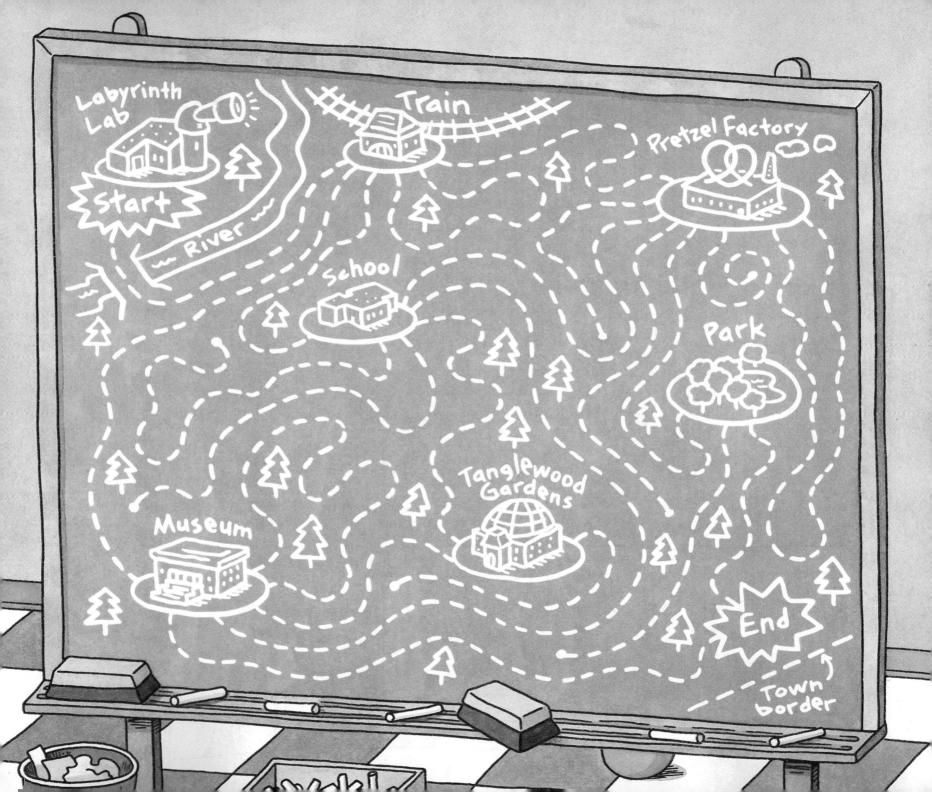

These three mazes may look like the world's easiest mazes, but if you try them, you'll find out otherwise. The trick is to draw one continuous line along each roadway (on the dotted lines) using *every* street only once. (You *can* cross over the same point twice.)

Well, isn't this a pickle! It looks as though the highway pavers have made the monumental mistake of filling the gas tanks of their highway paving machines with high-octane fuel. Now they can't stop the paving machines and roads are being paved everywhere! This is what we refer to in the scientific community as an R4I (or Run 4 It) situation.

Unfortunately, we need to get across town, and only one road will get us there. Can you find a way through this mess?

HILL DRILL

On the next page, we'll take a look inside an anthill. But first, we have to get there. Can you help me find the way to the anthill?

ANTY UP

It's nice to take in a little nature now and then. I make it a point to schedule in a couple of minutes every month.

A visit to this ant nest should do nicely for today. I've attached the X-ray screen onto the maze-o-scope so that we can get a better look at what goes on inside. Busy little hexapods (that's six-footed creatures for you non-scientists), aren't they?

Starting at the top of the anthill in the upper left, can you find a way through the ant nest to the anthill in the upper right? There are three ways, actually—one that goes through the Cornflake Chamber, one that goes through the Sleeping Chamber, and one that doesn't go through any chambers at all. Can you find all three?

MIND BENDER

How did these pretzels get like this? We'll get to that in a moment. In the meantime, can you find the two tangled twisters that are the same?

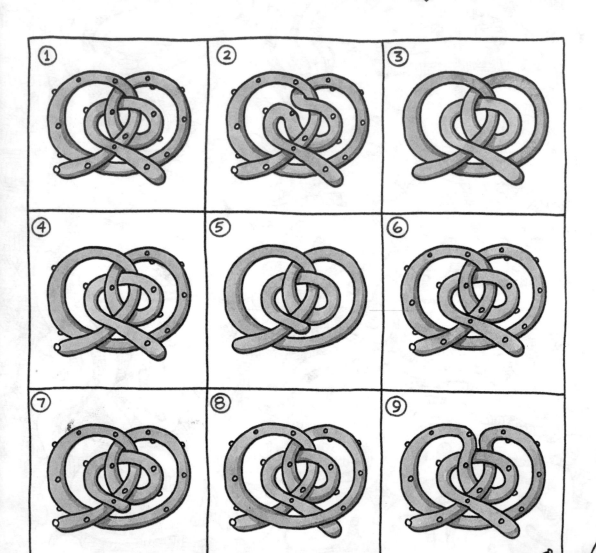

① ② ③
④ ⑤ ⑥
⑦ ⑧ ⑨

DO THE TWIST

"Shuddering salty snacks! Someone's been monkeying with the main computer at the pretzel factory. What kind of a twisted mind would dough...I mean...do such a thing!?!"

That's what I heard over the Maze Machine's radio as I drove through the north side of town. I wasn't far from the factory, so I decided to drive over and check it out. When I got there, I found a whole morning's worth of over-twisted pretzel output in the trash. I picked through the pile and found one particularly peculiar pretzel.

Can you find a path through this pretzel from "Start" to "Finish"?

Start

Finish

Tasty Twisters

ON THE RIGHT TRACK

Our town's railroad system has got to be the most confusing I've ever seen. Making it even worse is the fact that the trains can only go forward—not in reverse.

There's a train coming into the Moss Street Station that needs to get to the train yard. Can you help the engineer find the way?

You can go over the same stretch of track more than once, but remember—no backing up.

BACK STAGE

I heard they were shooting one of those disaster movies in town today, so I parked the Maze Machine and went over to watch the action. I'm glad I did because there was a crumbling hotel set that turned out to be a very interesting maze.

You'll find the set on the next two pages. On the left-hand page is the front of the set. On the right-hand page is the back of the set. Going back and forth between the two pages, can you get from "Start" to "End"? (No leaping or jumping from platforms allowed!)

Warning: A door that is on the left-hand side of the left-hand page will be on the right-hand side of the right-hand page. To avoid confusion, doorways have been lettered to help you go back and forth between the front and back.

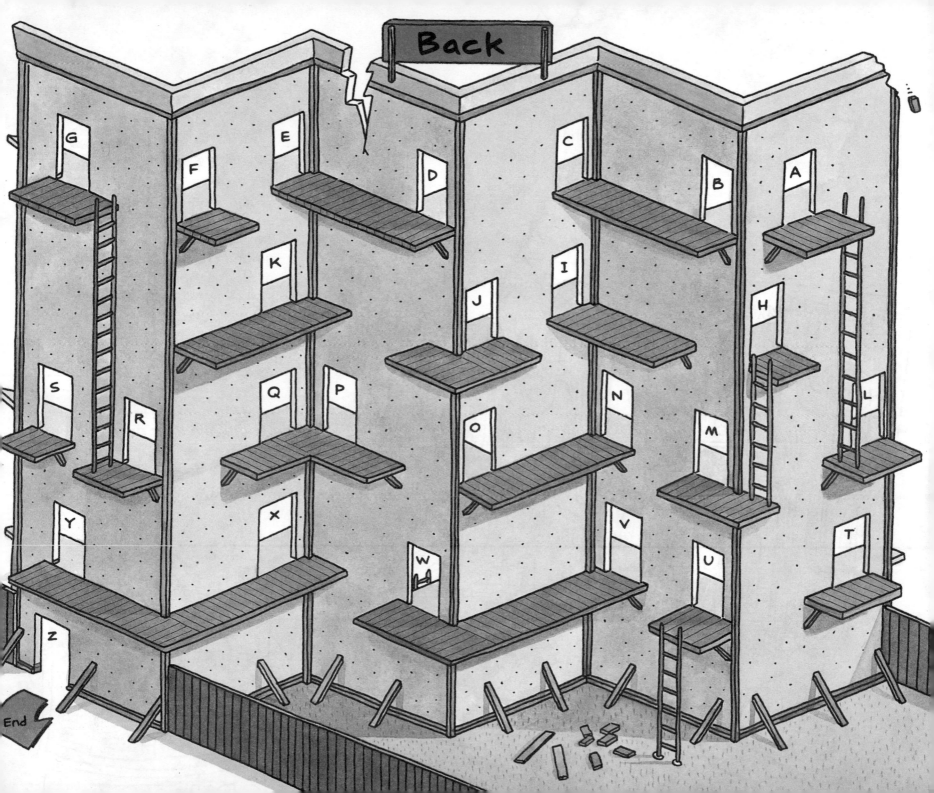

STICK
TO IT

As I pulled up to the corner of Yucca and Spine Streets, I saw this flyer. Starting at the bottom of the cactus, can you get to the top of its tallest arm? (You can go over and under branches.)

TRACKED US A
CACTUS

When I heard that the giant cacti were in bloom over at Tanglewood Gardens, I had to go and check it out. One look at the map inside the gardens, and I knew that this was my kind of place.

Take a look at the map yourself. Can you find two ways to get to the Cactus Exhibit? One way goes through the Baobab Grove—the other doesn't. (You can cross over the river where there are bridges.)

BRAIN DRAIN 15

I've programmed the Maze Machine's computer to create a "brain" maze for us. Moving one square at a time either up, down, left, or right (*but not diagonally*), can you find one B-R-A-I-N?

B	R	A	N	B	R	R	A
I	A	I	R	I	A	B	I
B	N	B	A	R	A	R	B
R	A	N	R	B	R	A	N
R	R	B	A	R	N	N	A
B	A	R	I	A	I	R	B

BRAIN BUSTER 16

I am often asked how the mazecracking mind works. The truth is I haven't the slightest idea.

I decided to feed all I know about mazecracking into the Maze Machine's central computer. The diagram on the next page is what I ended up with.

Starting at the eye, can you find what route an unsolved maze must make through the brain to get to the Maze-Solving Lobe?

Once you've found that path, can you find the route from the Maze-Solving Lobe down to the Line-Drawing Lobe?

Note: Brains can vary—do not be alarmed if yours is different from the one shown.

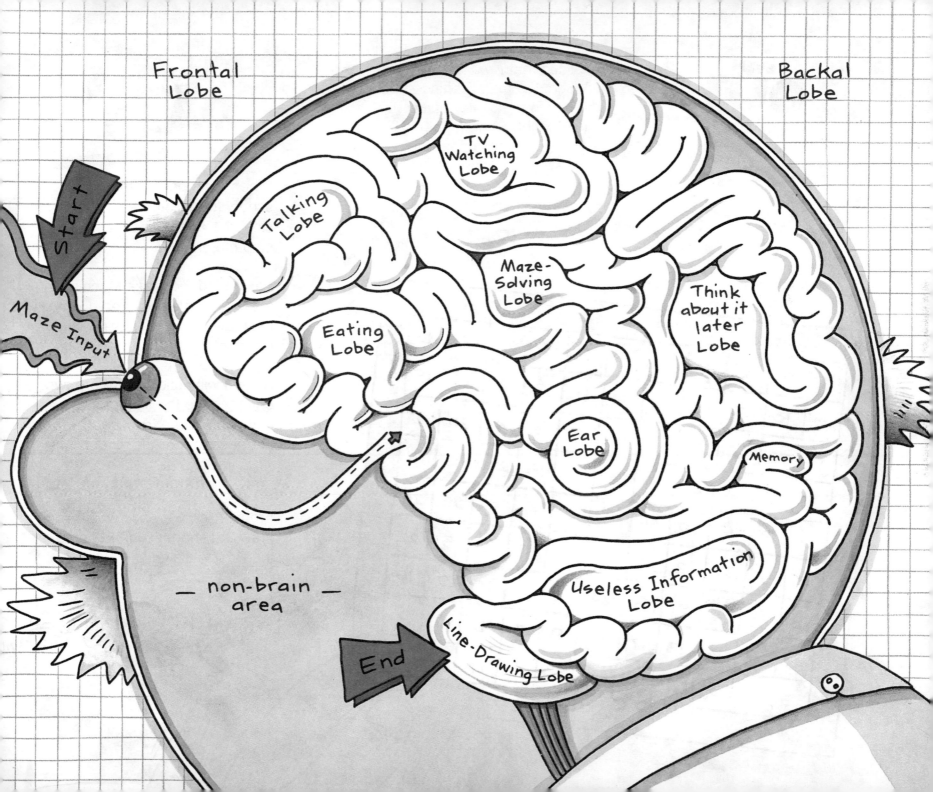

EVEN OUT

Below is a piece of paper I found on the ground outside the local school. As I looked it over,

I noticed that it was, oddly enough, a maze. Starting at the red box in the center of the page, can you find a path of *even* numbers that leads to one of the blue boxes? You can move up, down, left, or right, *but not diagonally*.

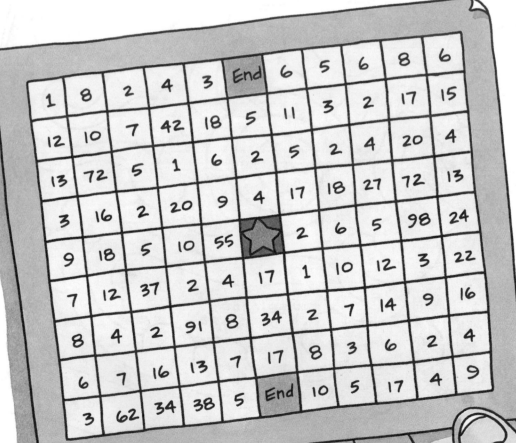

SCHOOL DAZE

When I stopped by the local school for a visit, I found it was closed. I wasn't about to let that stop me, though.

I extended the Maze Machine's scanner and discovered a very interesting floor plan inside the building.

As you will notice, there are two entrances to the school. Can you find a route from *each* entrance to the Auditorium?

Extra Credit

From which entrance would you draw the shortest line to get to the Principal's Office?

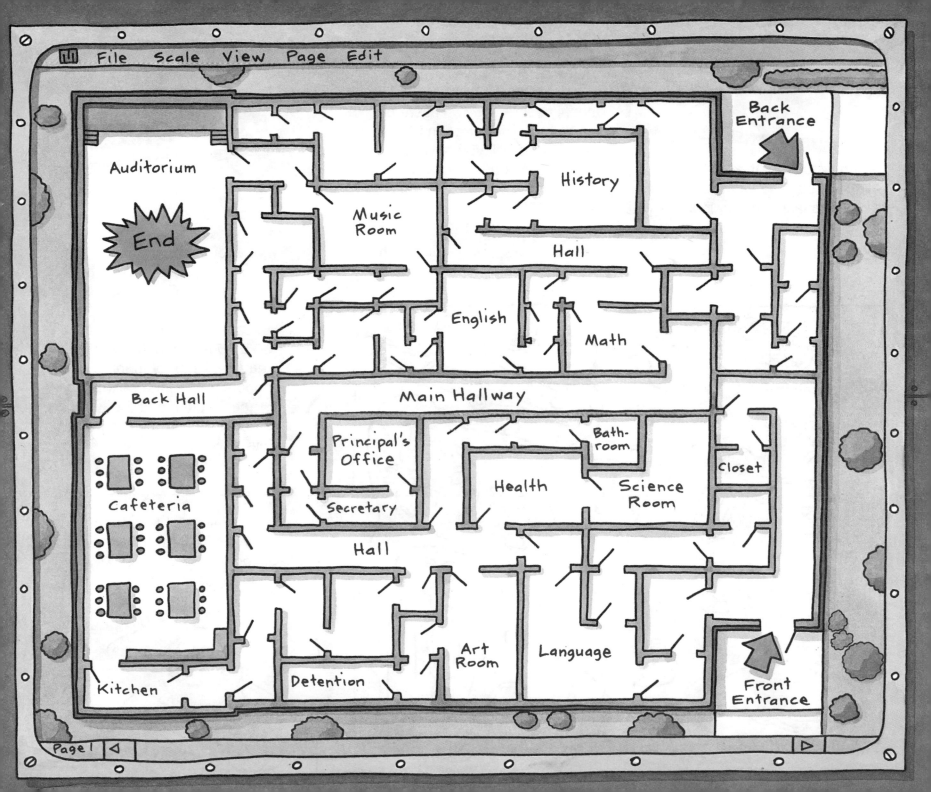

19 DON'T BLOW IT

As I drove by the local museum, this poster caught my eye. I pulled over to take a closer look. As you will notice, eight of the ten horns on the poster are tied together in pairs. Two aren't. Given enough tries, I'm sure you can figure out which two. The question is, how many horns will you have to pick before you know for sure?

2 or 3: a breeze
4: a little winded
5: blow hard

I hadn't visited the town museum for a while, so I decided to poke my head in and see what was new. You could have knocked me over with a noodle when I saw their new exhibit—a noodlehorn!

Because the tubing is so long on a noodlehorn, making one requires years of training. The noodlehorn on the next page is a good example of the work of a beginning noodlehorn maker—lots of wrong turns, dead ends, and wasted tubing.

Can you find the path a good puff of air must take to get from this noodlehorn's mouthpiece to its bell? (You can cross over and under tubing.)

Noodlehorn Exhibit

Horns of the World

The Shoehorn

NOW, SEE HERE

You may have noticed a rather jumbled array of mirrors on top of the Maze Machine. This is so I can see what I've just run over.

There are actually three different types of mirrors, and each one reflects things in a different way. All three are listed below. Can you figure out what image I will finally see when I look in the last mirror? 1. Will it be upside-down or right side up? 2. Will it be larger, smaller, or the same size? 3. Will it be reversed or not?

Hint: You may want to figure this out on a separate piece of paper.

1. Convex
3. Concave
5. Flat
7. Flat
2. Flat
4. Convex
6. Flat
8. Flat
9. Concave
11. Flat
10. Flat

The MAZE Machine

Dr. Knotts, Captain

All Mirrors: Reflection is reversed left to right.
Flat Mirror: Reflection is the same size.
Convex Mirror: Reflection is half size.
Concave Mirror: Reflection is double size & upside-down.

WHICH WAY

It's time to head back to the Labyrinth Lab, but it seems I made a wrong turn somewhere.

I stopped to ask for directions, but I don't think they are right. Can you figure out where I'll end up if I follow them? Starting at "Start," here they are:

1. Turn left at the 3rd light.
2. Go 2 blocks and turn left.
3. Turn right at the 2nd light.
4. Go 3 blocks and turn left.
5. Turn right at the 4th light.
6. It's the 1st building on the left after the 2nd light.

Driver's Test

What route *should* I have taken to get to the lab? Remember, you have to obey traffic signs—and you can't go through parking lots.

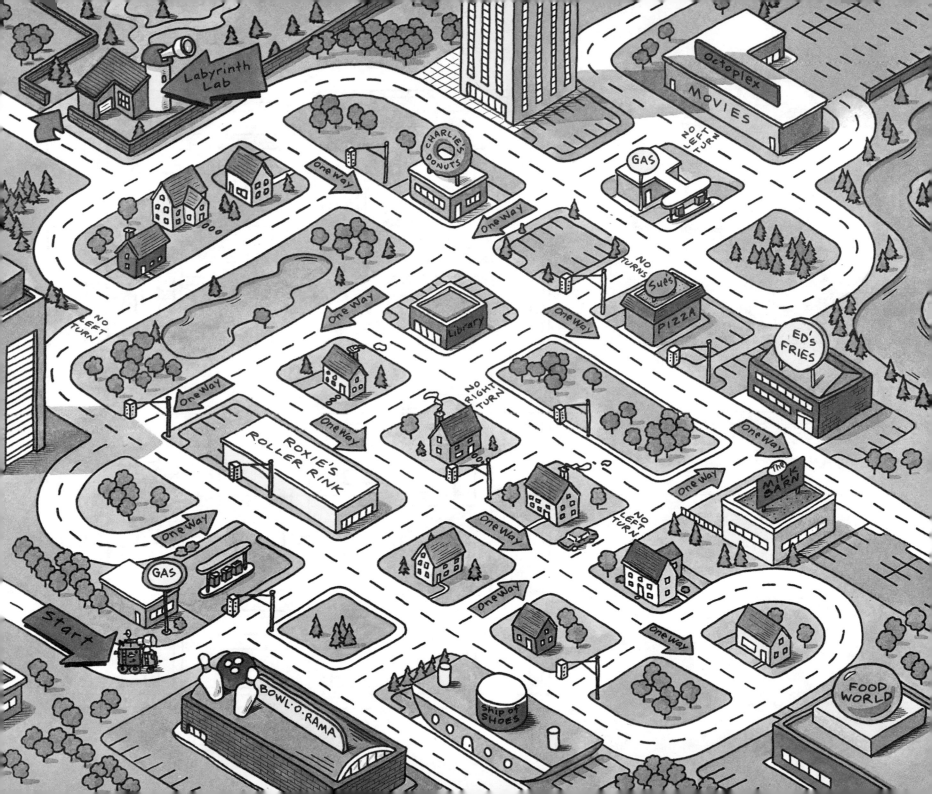

RAT RACE

23

Aaaaaaahhhh, home sweet lab! I think both the Maze Machine and I could use a rest after that mind-bending field trip.

Before you go, however, I have one last maze for you. It has been tested on the mice in my lab, and I have recorded their times below. How many of them can you beat?

Before you start, I think it's only fair to warn you that these mice have been bred and trained to crack the toughest mazes in record time. Still think you can beat them all? Time will tell....

Squealer: 1 minute 46 seconds
Lefty: 1 minute 3 seconds
Fuzzy: 51 seconds
Squeaky: 37 seconds
Whiskers: 24 seconds
Cheesy: 7 seconds!

ANSWERS

1. WHAT KNOTTS

His first name is GORDON.

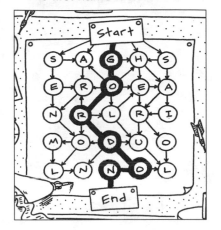

2. UNDER THE HOOD

6	Engine Starter
2	Wheel Activator
4	Maze-o-scope Controls
1	Horn
5	Radar Detector
3	Toaster Oven

4. CHALK IT UP

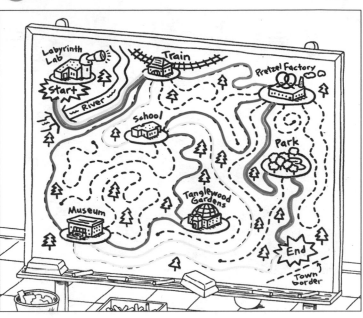

3. SEIZE THE KEYS

5. ROAD TEST

There are several ways to do each one. Here are ours:

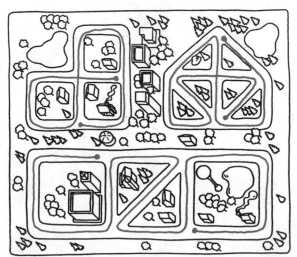

6

See next page.

7. HILL DRILL

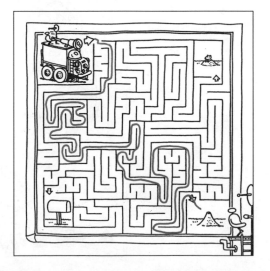

6 PAVE THE WAY

7

See previous page.

8 ANTY UP

9

MIND BENDER

Pretzels number 1 and 6 are the same.

10 DO THE TWIST

11 ON THE RIGHT TRACK

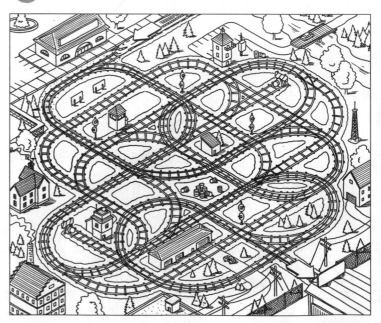

12 BACK STAGE

13

See next page.

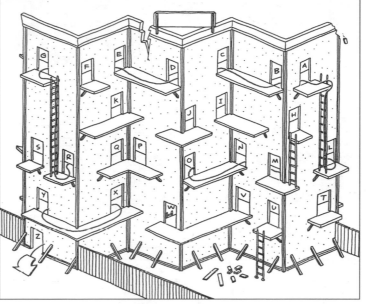

14 TRACKED US A CACTUS

15 See next page.

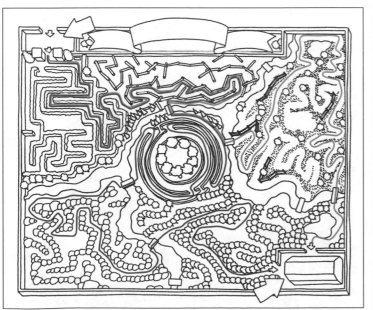

16 BRAIN BUSTER

17 18 See next page.

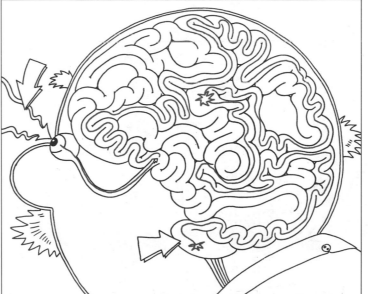

19 DON'T BLOW IT

Horn number 2 and horn number 10 are not tied together. Horn 1 is tied to horn 7. Horn 3 is tied to horn 6. Horn 4 is tied to horn 9. Horn 5 is tied to horn 8.

20

See next page.

21 NOW, SEE HERE

The image will be right side up, the same size, and reversed left to right.

13 STICK TO IT

15 BRAIN DRAIN

18 SCHOOL DAZE — The shortest route to the Principal's Office is from the back entrance.

17 EVEN OUT

23 RAT RACE

14 **16** **19** **21** See previous page.

20 USE YOUR NOODLE

22 WHICH WAY — The directions will take him to ED'S FRIES.

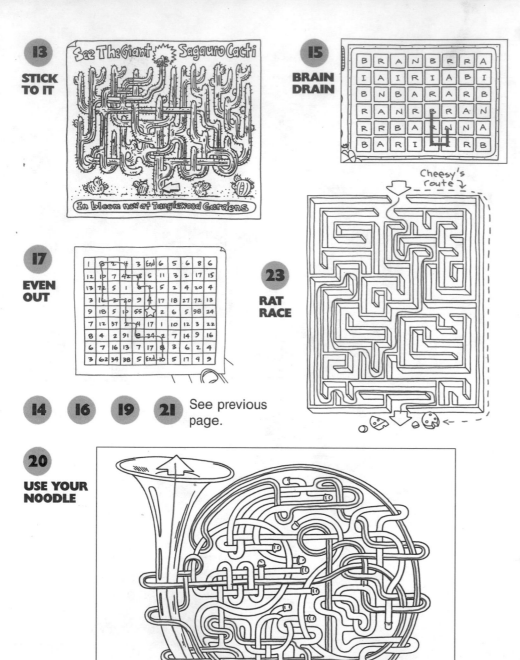
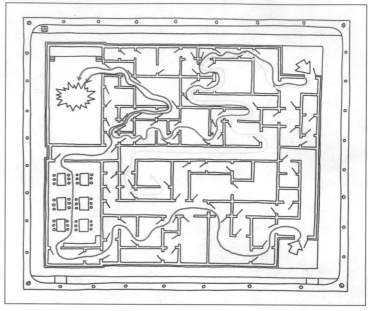
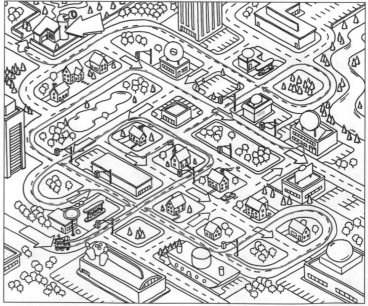